ALEXANDRA PAKHMUTOVA

CONCERTO

FOR TRUMPET AND ORCHESTRA

Reduction for Trumpet and Piano by Marcel G. Frank

Duration: 13:45 minutes

HAL•LEONARD®
CORPORATION

7777 W. BLUEMOUND RD. P.O. BOX 13819 MILWAUKEE, WI 53213

CONCERTO
For Trumpet and Orchestra

Reduction for Trumpet and Piano
By Marcel G. Frank

ALEXANDRA PAKHMUTOVA
(1955)

This work also available for Trumpet and Band.

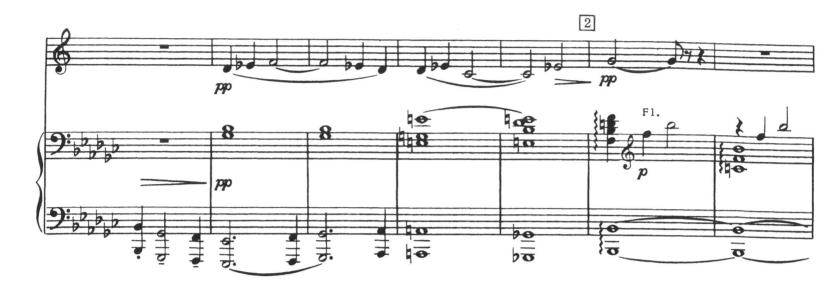

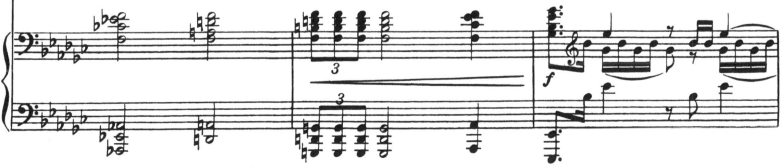

9

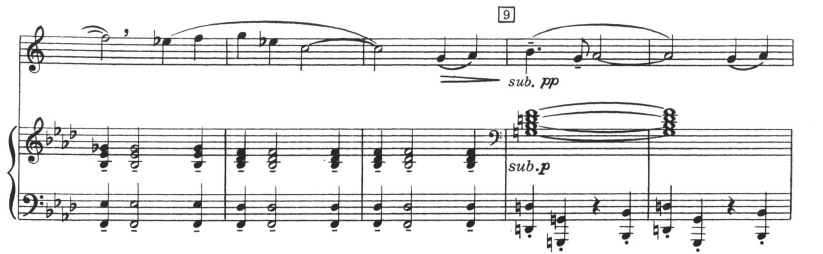

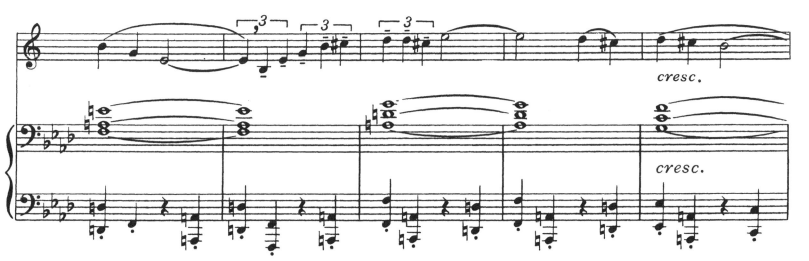

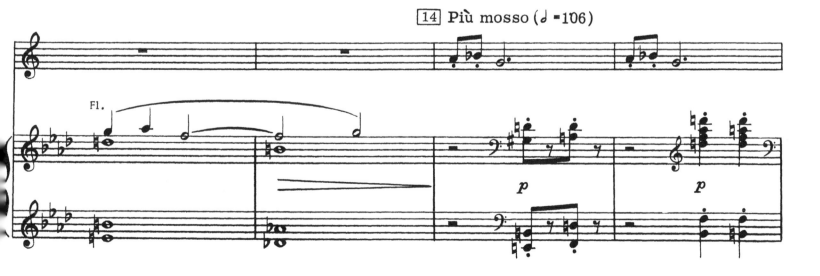

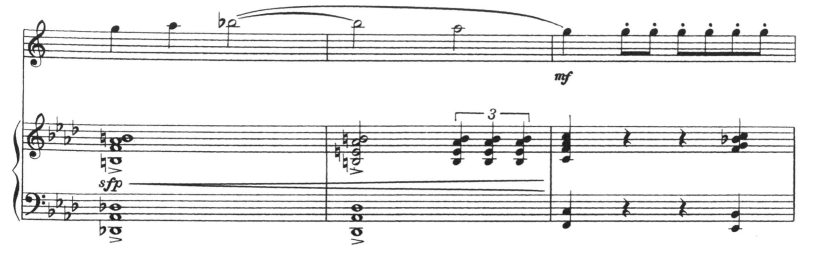

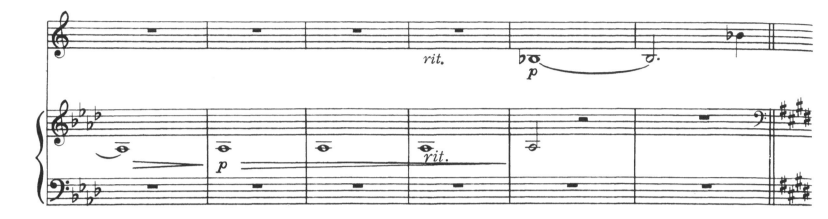

16 Adagio (♩ =58)

dolce

Ob.

20 Tempo I (Allegro)

19

CONCERTO
For Trumpet and Orchestra

Trumpet in B♭

ALEXANDRA PAKHMUTOVA
(1955)

Andante (♩=63)

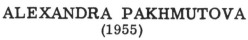

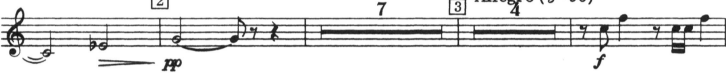

This work also available for Trumpet and Band.

Trumpet in B♭

Trumpet in B♭

Adagio (♩=58)

Più mosso (♩=88)

poco a poco accelerando

Tempo I (Allegro)

Trumpet in B♭

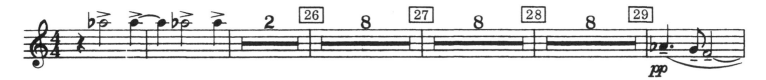

Trumpet in B♭

Trumpet in B♭

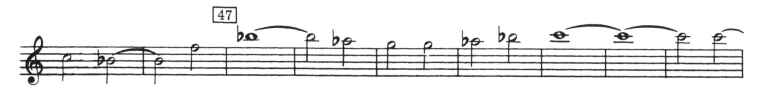

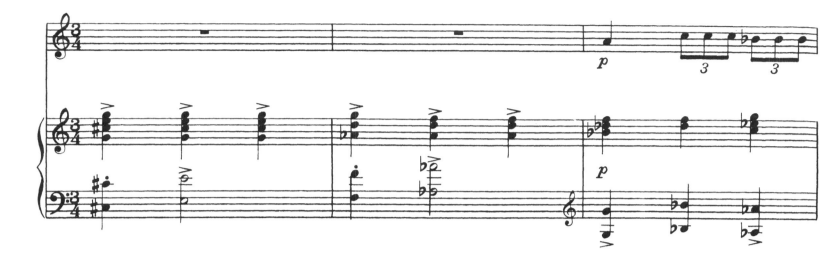

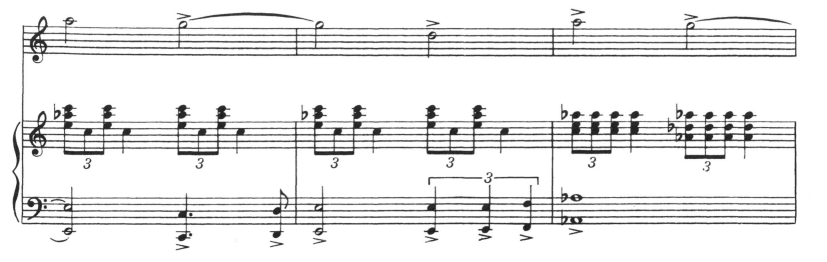

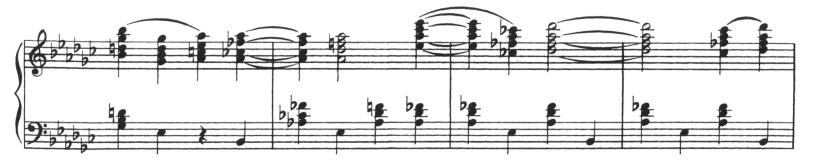

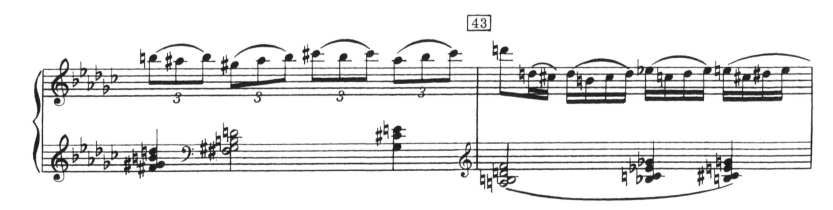

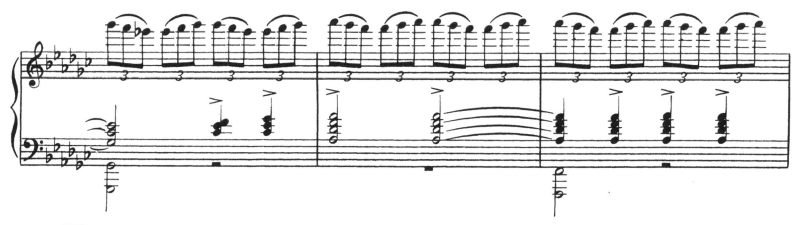

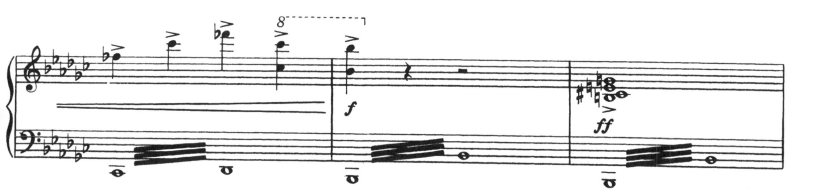

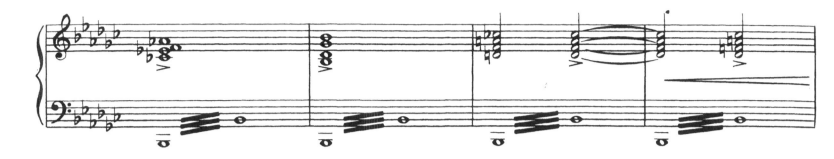

46 Maestoso (♩=86)

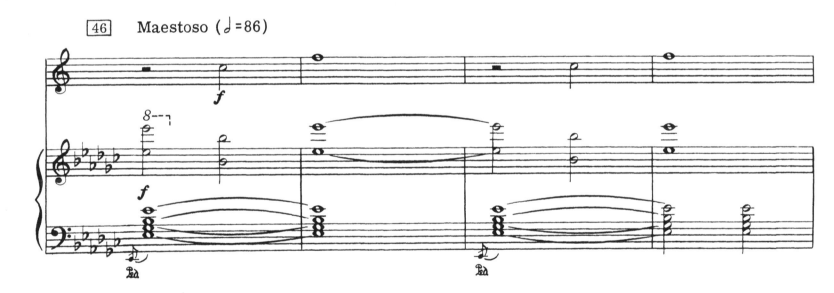

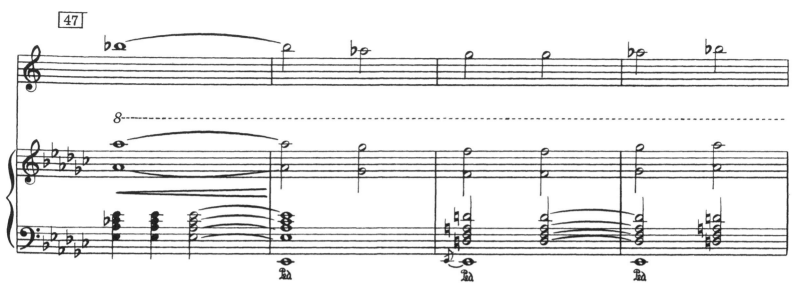

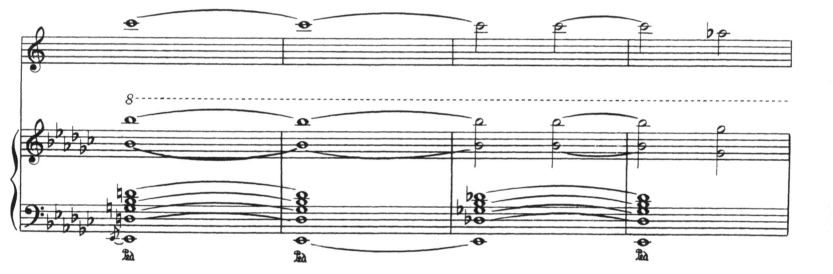

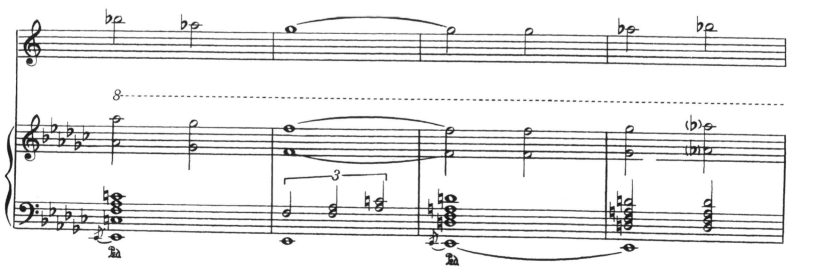

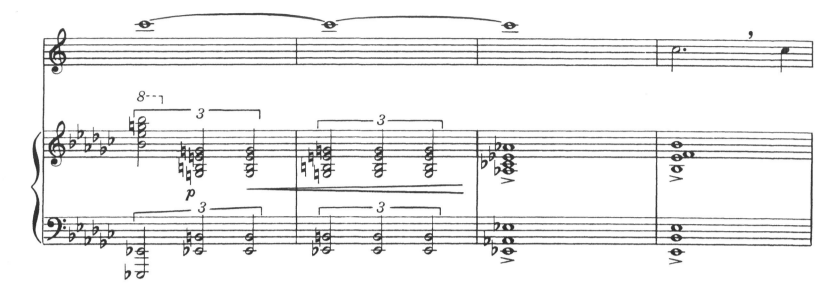

Molto Allegro

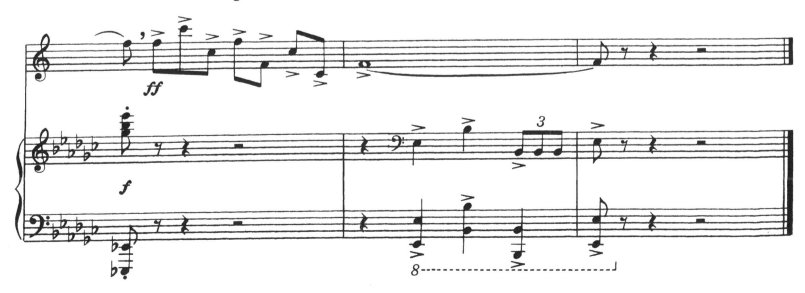